INSIDE THE ROG ALLY X

A Complete Guide to the Handheld Gaming Experience

The Story, Performance, and What Every Buyer Needs to Know Before Choosing

Tom K. Smith

Table of Contents

Introduction

Gaming has always had a special place in the hearts of many, especially those who grew up with handheld devices like the Game Boy. There was something magical about having a world of entertainment right in your hands, whether it was a long road trip, a quick break between chores, or even just a few stolen moments while waiting in line. These devices weren't just about the games themselves—they became a gateway to shared experiences and memories, like trading Pokémon with friends at school using the Game Boy Link cable. The simplicity and accessibility of these early handhelds made them an inseparable part of many childhoods, creating a deep, lasting connection to gaming.

As the years passed, life inevitably became busier. The responsibilities of work, family, and everyday life began to take priority, leaving less and less time for those long, immersive gaming sessions. But for many, the desire to escape into a game never really faded. The challenge became finding a way to fit gaming into a busy schedule without sacrificing the joy and excitement that comes with it.

Enter the ROG Ally X, a handheld gaming device that promises to bring that spark of joy back to gamers who may have thought their gaming days were behind them. This book takes an in-depth look at what makes the ROG Ally X such a compelling choice, particularly for casual gamers who crave the flexibility to enjoy their favorite games whenever they can find a few moments.

Through a detailed exploration of its features, performance, and design, this book aims to uncover why the ROG Ally X stands out in a crowded market of gaming devices. Whether you're looking for an introduction to handheld gaming or considering a new addition to your collection, this guide will provide you with the insights and information you need to make an informed choice.

Chapter 1: The Unboxing Experience

The excitement of unboxing a new gadget is something that never gets old, and the ROG Ally X doesn't disappoint in this regard. From the moment the package is opened, it's clear that this device was designed to impress. Nestled securely inside the box is the ROG Ally X, a sleek and polished piece of tech that feels both modern and familiar, with subtle nods to the handheld gaming consoles of the past.

Alongside the device, you'll find the essentials: a 65W charger, a set of manuals, and a small warranty card. Asus has also included a flimsy but functional device stand, tucked away at the top of the box—a small addition that, while not particularly sturdy, serves its purpose. The stand may not be the highlight of the unboxing experience, but it's a nice touch to have something included, considering the price point.

As you hold the device for the first time, the weight and build of the ROG Ally X immediately stand out.

It's lighter than expected, making it comfortable to hold for extended gaming sessions, yet it still feels substantial and solid. Every detail, from the ergonomic design to the placement of buttons and joysticks, has been carefully thought through, making the first impression a strong one.

However, just as you're about to dive into the setup, there's a small hiccup. A faint rattling sound can be heard from inside the unit—an unsettling discovery, to say the least. It feels as though a tiny piece of plastic or some foreign object might have been sealed within the device during manufacturing. This unexpected noise leaves a lingering doubt, but the hope is that it's just a minor, isolated issue. For now, the focus shifts back to the setup and getting the device ready to play.

The initial unboxing of the ROG Ally X, despite the small hiccup, sets the stage for what promises to be a gaming experience that combines the nostalgia of handheld devices with the power and performance of modern gaming technology.

The excitement of unboxing the ROG Ally X was momentarily overshadowed by an unexpected discovery—a faint rattling sound coming from within the device. It was a concerning noise, something that shouldn't be part of a brand-new piece of technology. The mind races to consider the possibilities: could it be a loose component? A fragment of plastic left behind during assembly?

Despite the unsettling sound, the decision was made to move forward with the setup, hoping that the issue was more of an annoyance than a real problem. Days passed, and the rattling persisted intermittently. It was a nagging reminder of the initial concern, but surprisingly, the noise eventually disappeared on its own. Whether it was a small piece of plastic that lodged itself into place or simply a fluke, the issue resolved without intervention.

This experience serves as a reminder that even the most well-designed devices can have small imperfections, and while the rattling noise could have been a more significant problem, it ended up being just a minor bump in an otherwise smooth journey with the ROG Ally X.

Setting up the ROG Ally X is where the excitement of unboxing quickly transitions into the reality of getting the device ready for use. Since it runs on Windows 11, the setup process is much like configuring a new PC. This brings with it both familiarity and some initial frustration. The standard steps are all there: signing into your Microsoft account, agreeing to terms, setting up passwords, and connecting to Wi-Fi. But unlike a gaming console, which is designed for quick and easy setup, this handheld gaming device feels more like you're booting up a laptop for the first time.

Once the account is created and initial settings are completed, the next task is dealing with updates. Windows 11, like any modern operating system, is constantly evolving, so downloading and installing updates is inevitable. While this ensures that the system is running smoothly with the latest security patches, it also adds time to the setup process—time that could be spent gaming.

In addition to updates, there's the matter of bloatware. Like many new Windows devices, the ROG Ally X comes preloaded with apps and programs that may not be relevant to gaming. News apps, trial versions of software, and even ads for services clutter the system, creating unnecessary distractions. Removing this bloatware becomes an essential step in optimizing the device for gaming. It's not a particularly enjoyable task, but it's necessary to free up resources and create a streamlined experience.

Despite these initial hurdles, once the device is cleaned up and fully updated, it's ready to show off what it can really do. Setting up the ROG Ally X may require more time and patience than a typical gaming console, but it's a small trade-off for the power and flexibility that come with having a full-fledged Windows 11 system in the palm of your hand.

Chapter 2: The Display and Visuals

The ROG Ally X truly shines when it comes to its display. At the heart of the device is a 7-inch, 120Hz IPS LCD screen that immediately sets the tone for an immersive gaming experience. The display is vibrant, delivering sharp images and smooth motion, which is crucial for both casual gaming and more graphically demanding titles. The resolution, while not quite at the level of a top-tier desktop monitor, still impresses with its clarity and brightness. Whether you're navigating a beautifully crafted open-world environment or engaged in the fast-paced action of a racing game, the screen handles everything with ease.

One of the most notable features of this display is the 120Hz refresh rate. This high refresh rate makes a significant difference, especially in fast-motion games where fluidity is key. Actions feel more responsive, and there's a noticeable reduction in screen tearing and motion blur. This level of performance in a handheld device makes it a serious contender against other gaming systems, particularly for those who value smooth gameplay.

The IPS technology also plays a role in enhancing the visual experience. It provides consistent color accuracy and wide viewing angles, so no matter how you're holding the device, the picture quality remains solid. The colors are rich, and the contrast is well-balanced, making both bright and dark scenes pop on the screen.

While the display performs exceptionally well for its size, there's always room for improvement. An OLED screen, for instance, could take the visuals to another level by offering deeper blacks and even more vibrant colors. But for now, the IPS LCD display on the ROG Ally X holds its own, providing a strong balance between quality and performance that elevates handheld gaming to a new standard.

The ROG Ally X's 7-inch, 120Hz IPS LCD screen plays a pivotal role in enhancing the overall gaming experience, regardless of the type of game you're playing. Across various genres, the display showcases its versatility. For art-focused games with intricate environments and detailed textures, like *The Long Dark*, the screen does an impressive job of bringing the visuals to life. The colors are rich and nuanced, capturing the beauty of the game's landscapes and subtle details that might be lost on a lesser display. The IPS technology ensures that the colors remain vibrant, even from wide viewing angles, so you can appreciate the artwork of these games no matter how you're holding the device.

When it comes to fast-paced action games, such as *F1* or *Halo Infinite*, the 120Hz refresh rate becomes a game-changer. The higher refresh rate smooths out the action, making rapid movements feel more fluid and responsive. Whether you're speeding around a track or engaged in a firefight, the screen keeps up with the fast motion, delivering a gaming experience that feels closer to what you'd expect from a desktop gaming setup than a handheld device. This makes the ROG Ally X stand out, especially for those who prefer action-packed gameplay where every millisecond counts.

When comparing the ROG Ally X to other handheld devices like the Nintendo Switch, the difference in display quality is immediately noticeable. The Switch's 720p display, while adequate for many games, simply doesn't offer the same level of sharpness and fluidity as the ROG Ally X's 120Hz IPS screen. Colors on the Ally X appear more vibrant, and the higher resolution provides clearer visuals, making everything from small text to fine details easier to see. The smoother gameplay enabled by the 120Hz refresh rate also gives the Ally X an edge, particularly in games where performance can make or break the experience.

However, despite the strengths of the IPS LCD display, there is still room for future improvement. An OLED screen, for example, could elevate the visual experience even further. With its ability to produce deeper blacks and more vivid colors, OLED technology would enhance both the visual fidelity and the overall immersion in games. The contrast ratio of OLED screens is unmatched, making dark scenes look richer and more realistic. While the ROG Ally X's current display is impressive, the possibility of an OLED upgrade in future iterations would certainly be a welcome enhancement, especially for gamers who crave the best possible visual experience in a handheld device.

Chapter 3: Hardware and Performance

At the core of the ROG Ally X lies some seriously powerful hardware, making it more than just a casual gaming device. The AMD Ryzen Z1 Extreme chip is the star of the show, providing the processing power needed to handle a wide range of games, from indie titles to AAA blockbusters. This chip is built for gaming, boasting enough performance to push high frame rates and deliver smooth gameplay, even in more demanding titles. Paired with the 24GB of LPDDR5X RAM, the ROG Ally X is well-equipped to multitask and handle resource-intensive games without breaking a sweat.

The combination of the Ryzen Z1 Extreme chip and the ample RAM allows the device to tackle modern games at medium settings, often hitting a comfortable 30 frames per second or more, depending on the game and settings. For a handheld device, this is an impressive feat, bringing console-quality gaming into a portable format. The increased memory also helps ensure that background tasks, such as game updates or system processes, don't interfere with gameplay, providing a smoother overall experience.

Beyond the processor and RAM, the ROG Ally X comes with other hardware features that further enhance its performance. The device is equipped with a fast SSD, which not only reduces load times but also allows for quick access to games and applications. The built-in Wi-Fi ensures a strong and stable connection for online play, and the integrated cooling system helps keep the device from overheating during extended gaming sessions. Additionally, the Ally X offers a range of customizable options, allowing gamers to tweak performance settings to optimize battery life, frame rates, or visuals based on their current needs.

These hardware specs make the ROG Ally X a serious contender in the handheld gaming market. It's not just about portability; it's about delivering a gaming experience that's on par with what you'd expect from a larger, more powerful device.

Whether you're playing the latest releases or revisiting old favorites, the Ally X is built to perform, and it does so with impressive consistency.

The ROG Ally X proves that handheld gaming devices can handle more than just casual or retro titles—it's built to tackle AAA games head-on. The combination of the AMD Ryzen Z1 Extreme chip and 24GB of RAM allows the device to run demanding games at respectable settings, often delivering performance levels that would have seemed impossible for a portable console just a few years ago. Games like *F1* showcase the device's ability to maintain high frame rates, often exceeding 100 frames per second, making the gameplay feel smooth and responsive, which is essential for such fast-paced action. The 120Hz display further amplifies this experience, making everything look seamless, even when the speed is cranked up.

However, it's not just racing games that the ROG Ally X excels at. Titles like *Forza Motorsport* show how well this device can manage more graphically intense games. While playing at medium settings and targeting a 900p or 1080p resolution, the performance remains steady, with the device consistently delivering 30 frames per second or higher. There are occasional hiccups—*Forza Motorsport*, for example, has been known to crash at specific points, but this seems to be more of a game issue than a problem with the Ally X itself. For the most part, the device handles these heavy hitters with grace, making it a solid option for gamers who don't want to be tied down to a desk or a console.

One of the standout features of the ROG Ally X is the level of customizability it offers. Gamers are given control over how the device operates, allowing them to tweak performance settings to find the perfect balance between visuals, battery life, and frame rates. This flexibility is particularly useful for a handheld device, where battery conservation is often just as important as performance.

At the heart of this customizability is the Command Center. This easy-to-access menu allows players to adjust various settings on the fly. Whether it's locking frame rates, enabling AMD's FSR (FidelityFX Super Resolution) for better performance at lower resolutions, or fine-tuning in-game graphical settings, the Command Center makes it possible to optimize the gaming experience in real time. Players can quickly switch between performance modes depending on their needs, such as prioritizing battery life when on the go or maximizing performance when plugged in at home. For those who prefer not to spend too much time tweaking, there are also pre-configured settings shared by the community, ensuring that finding the right setup for each game is both easy and effective.

This level of control means that whether you're playing an intense AAA game or something lighter, the ROG Ally X can be tailored to suit your preferences. It's this adaptability that makes it stand out in the world of handheld gaming, offering a gaming experience that can be as powerful or as energy-efficient as you need it to be.

Chapter 4: Comfort and Ergonomics

The ROG Ally X has taken significant steps forward in design, building on the strengths of its predecessor while addressing some of the pain points that gamers had with the original model. One of the most noticeable improvements is the ergonomics of the device. The grip has been redesigned with a rounder, more natural shape that better conforms to the hand. This simple yet effective change makes a big difference during extended gaming sessions, reducing hand fatigue and making the device feel more comfortable to hold over long periods.

The joysticks have also received an upgrade. They are now full-sized with a deeper concave, which provides a more secure and comfortable resting spot for the thumbs. This might seem like a small detail, but it has a huge impact on gameplay, particularly for titles that require precision and quick movements. The new design minimizes slipping and ensures that players can maintain control, even during the most intense moments. Additionally, the joysticks feel sturdy and responsive, giving the player a greater sense of control over in-game actions.

Another area where the ROG Ally X has seen significant improvement is in its buttons. The triggers and bumpers are now more satisfying to press, with a tactile feel that gamers will appreciate. Whether you're mashing buttons in an arcade-style fighter or methodically pressing them during a strategy game, the response is immediate and reliable. The larger D-pad is another thoughtful addition, particularly for fans of retro-style games or fighting games, where precise directional input is critical. Unlike smaller D-pads, which can feel cramped and unresponsive, the one on the Ally X is sharp and well-positioned, making it easier to execute moves accurately.

All these design improvements contribute to a more refined and enjoyable gaming experience. The ROG Ally X feels like a device that was crafted with the player in mind, focusing on making every aspect of the hardware more intuitive and comfortable to use. This attention to detail elevates it from just another handheld gaming device to something that truly enhances the experience of gaming on the go.

When diving into extended gaming sessions with the ROG Ally X, the improvements in design become even more apparent. The rounder grip and thoughtfully placed controls make it easy to settle in for a long playthrough without constantly adjusting your hands or feeling the strain. The device's lighter weight also plays a role here, making it easier to hold for longer periods without causing fatigue. Whether you're stretched out on the couch or sitting in a less-than-ideal posture, the ROG Ally X manages to maintain a comfortable feel throughout your session.

The full-sized joysticks, with their deep concave design, provide a solid grip that makes gameplay feel more controlled and precise. During high-action moments, when quick reflexes are crucial, the joysticks respond smoothly and allow for precise movement without causing strain on the thumbs. This thoughtful ergonomic design is a significant upgrade, as it feels natural, and over time, it becomes clear that the device was built with comfort in mind.

However, comfort is ultimately subjective and can vary greatly depending on individual preferences and hand size. What feels perfect for one gamer might not work as well for another. For those with larger hands, the ROG Ally X's design may feel just right, with controls that are easy to reach and buttons that are satisfyingly responsive. On the other hand, someone with smaller hands might find the device a bit bulky or struggle to comfortably reach all the buttons without adjusting their grip.

The subjectivity of comfort means that no one-size-fits-all solution exists in handheld gaming, and while the ROG Ally X makes commendable strides in accommodating a wide range of gamers, personal experiences will inevitably differ. The key takeaway is that the device's design is focused on reducing the strain that typically comes with extended gameplay. It may not be perfect for everyone, but it's a significant step forward in making handheld gaming more accessible and enjoyable for a broader audience.

Chapter 5: Battery Life and Power Management

The ROG Ally X comes equipped with a substantial 80W battery, which marks a significant upgrade from the 40W battery found in its predecessor. This increase in capacity directly impacts the device's ability to sustain longer gaming sessions without frequent recharges, a critical improvement for gamers who are often on the go. With double the battery power, the Ally X can now handle more demanding tasks while offering a more consistent and reliable gaming experience.

The expanded battery capacity provides users with greater flexibility. When running intensive AAA games at higher settings, you can still expect around two hours of gameplay before needing to recharge. This is a significant improvement over the previous model, which struggled to keep up with such demands. For less demanding games or when the device is set to lower power modes like Silent or Performance mode, the battery can stretch even further, delivering up to eight to ten hours of gameplay on a single charge. This versatility makes the Ally X a more appealing choice for those who travel frequently or enjoy gaming in short bursts throughout the day.

While the increased battery capacity is a welcome improvement, it also comes with some considerations. Battery life still varies greatly depending on the type of game being played and the performance settings chosen. For instance, when pushing the device to its limits in Turbo mode, which prioritizes performance over battery life, the longevity of the charge diminishes. However, the ability to switch between different power modes gives users more control over how they balance performance and battery efficiency.

In comparison to its predecessor, the 80W battery of the ROG Ally X feels like a necessary evolution. Where the previous model struggled with longevity, the Ally X takes a step forward in offering a more reliable and user-friendly experience. This improvement underscores Asus's commitment to addressing the practical needs of gamers who expect their handheld devices to last longer and perform better, making the ROG Ally X a more viable option for those who prioritize battery life without sacrificing performance.

The ROG Ally X offers a range of power modes that allow gamers to tailor the device's performance and battery life to suit their needs. These modes—Silent, Performance, and Turbo—each serve a specific purpose, helping users find the right balance between conserving battery power and maximizing gaming performance.

Silent mode is designed for those moments when battery efficiency is the top priority. It limits the device's power consumption to 13W, reducing the overall performance but significantly extending battery life. This mode is ideal for lighter games that don't require a lot of processing power or when you're just using the device for basic tasks, such as browsing or watching videos. In Silent mode, you can stretch the battery life to its fullest potential, with some lighter games running for up to eight to ten hours on a single charge.

Performance mode is the middle ground, offering a balance between power and efficiency. At 17W, this mode still prioritizes battery life but allows for better performance than Silent mode, making it suitable for most games. In real-world use, Performance mode is perfect for gaming sessions that require moderate graphical power without draining the battery too quickly. For many gamers, this mode will likely be the go-to setting, as it provides a good mix of smooth gameplay and reasonable battery longevity, usually offering around four to five hours of gaming, depending on the game's demands.

Turbo mode is where the ROG Ally X really flexes its muscles, pushing the hardware to its limits by maximizing power output. This mode is best suited for demanding AAA titles that require higher performance levels to run smoothly. When plugged in, Turbo mode unleashes the full potential of the device, delivering top-tier performance with frame rates and visual fidelity that rival those of more traditional gaming setups. However, when running on battery alone, Turbo mode naturally comes with a cost—battery life can be as short as two hours, especially for graphically intensive games. This mode is best used when gaming sessions are short, or when the device is plugged into a power source.

In practical use, the flexibility of these power modes becomes a valuable tool for gamers. For example, while playing a demanding game like *Halo Infinite* on Turbo mode, the experience is smooth and responsive, but the battery life drains quickly, making it ideal for short bursts of intense gaming or when near a charger. On the other hand, switching to Silent or Performance mode for a less demanding game like *Stardew Valley* or *Hades* allows for much longer sessions, making it easier to game for extended periods without worrying about finding an outlet.

The variety of power modes offered by the ROG Ally X gives users the ability to tailor their gaming experience based on their environment and priorities. Whether you're looking to conserve battery while traveling or pushing the device to its full potential during a high-stakes gaming session, the ROG Ally X adapts to meet your needs, making it a versatile and powerful tool for handheld gaming.

Chapter 6: Competing Devices

In the competitive world of handheld gaming devices, the ROG Ally X stands out for its powerful hardware and customization options, but it faces stiff competition from other well-established players like the Steam Deck and the upcoming Legion Go. Each device has its own strengths and weaknesses, making the choice largely dependent on a gamer's specific needs and preferences.

The Steam Deck, one of the most talked-about handhelds in recent years, is a strong competitor to the ROG Ally X. It runs SteamOS, which is designed from the ground up for gaming, offering a more seamless experience for gamers who primarily use Steam for their library. The simplicity of SteamOS makes the Deck more user-friendly in many respects, eliminating much of the setup complexity and bloatware that comes with Windows 11 on the Ally X. The Steam Deck also benefits from tighter integration with Valve's ecosystem, which is a major selling point for players who want an optimized gaming experience without the need to tweak settings manually.

However, the Steam Deck lags behind the ROG Ally X in terms of raw performance. The Ally X's AMD Ryzen Z1 Extreme chip and 24GB of RAM outpace the Steam Deck's custom AMD APU, especially when it comes to handling demanding AAA titles. The ROG Ally X's 120Hz display also provides a smoother gaming experience compared to the Steam Deck's 60Hz screen, which can make a noticeable difference in fast-paced games. The higher refresh rate and more powerful hardware give the ROG Ally X an edge for gamers who value performance and visual fidelity in a handheld device.

The Legion Go, on the other hand, brings its own set of features to the table. Lenovo's handheld is designed with a focus on versatility, offering detachable controllers similar to the Nintendo Switch. This modular approach appeals to gamers who want the flexibility of different play styles, whether handheld or docked. The Legion Go also boasts a competitive hardware setup, with its own version of AMD's latest mobile chips, which positions it alongside the ROG Ally X in terms of performance. Additionally, the Legion Go's software experience is built around Lenovo's own ecosystem, which promises smoother integration with other Lenovo products.

In terms of display, the ROG Ally X's 7-inch, 120Hz IPS LCD screen provides a more premium experience compared to both the Steam Deck and Legion Go, particularly in terms of refresh rate and overall visual quality. While the Legion Go offers a large screen with solid performance, its refresh rate lags behind that of the Ally X, making the Asus device more appealing to gamers who prioritize smooth visuals. The Steam Deck, while solid in its own right, can't compete with the sharpness and fluidity of the Ally X's display.

Price is another factor where the Steam Deck has an advantage. At a lower starting price point, it offers a more affordable entry into handheld gaming for those who may not need the extra horsepower or features of the ROG Ally X. The Legion Go is expected to fall somewhere in between, offering a balance of price and performance, but still positioned as a premium device.

Ultimately, the ROG Ally X is a top contender for gamers who want a high-performance handheld experience with the flexibility of Windows 11, even if it requires more setup and customization. The Steam Deck remains the go-to choice for simplicity and affordability, especially for Steam-centric gamers, while the Legion Go offers an innovative middle ground with its detachable controllers and versatile design. Each device has its own appeal, and the right choice depends on what matters most to the gamer—performance, ease of use, or versatility.

The ROG Ally X stands as a formidable option in the handheld gaming market, but like any device, it comes with its own set of strengths and weaknesses when compared to its competition.

Strengths:

One of the ROG Ally X's biggest advantages over competitors like the Steam Deck and Legion Go is its sheer performance power. The AMD Ryzen Z1 Extreme chip, coupled with 24GB of RAM, gives the Ally X the ability to handle AAA games at medium to high settings with smooth frame rates, often surpassing the capabilities of other handhelds. This makes it an appealing choice for gamers who prioritize performance and want a device that can tackle the most demanding titles on the go.

The 120Hz IPS LCD display is another standout feature. While the Steam Deck and Legion Go offer solid screens, the 120Hz refresh rate on the Ally X provides a much smoother visual experience, particularly in fast-paced games. The higher refresh rate, combined with the bright and sharp 7-inch display, sets it apart from its competitors in terms of visual fluidity and overall gaming experience.

Customizability is another strength. The ROG Ally X allows users to tweak performance settings, offering control over how the device balances battery life and graphical performance. The Command Center makes it easy to adjust settings on the fly, giving gamers flexibility based on their specific gaming needs. This level of control is a significant advantage for players who want to optimize their device for different types of games or situations.

Weaknesses:

However, the ROG Ally X isn't without its drawbacks. The most significant weakness is the setup process. Running Windows 11 on a handheld device brings a level of complexity that many gamers may find frustrating. From dealing with bloatware to navigating a desktop operating system on a portable console, the experience can feel cumbersome compared to the streamlined gaming-focused OS on the Steam Deck. SteamOS, with its ease of use and seamless integration with the Steam library, offers a more polished and user-friendly experience for those who want to jump straight into gaming without the hassle of tweaking settings or managing a full Windows environment.

Another area where the ROG Ally X lags is its software ecosystem. While Windows 11 provides versatility, it lacks the gaming-specific focus of SteamOS. The Armory Crate software, while functional, doesn't quite measure up to the fluidity of SteamOS, which was designed specifically for gaming. This difference can be noticeable, especially for gamers used to the plug-and-play simplicity of consoles.

Additionally, despite the increased battery capacity, the ROG Ally X still struggles with battery life when running in Turbo mode or playing more demanding games. While the different power modes help extend battery life, the device can still drain quickly when pushed to its limits. Gamers who prioritize long, uninterrupted gaming sessions might find themselves needing to charge more often than they'd like.

Price Considerations:

At a price point of $799, the ROG Ally X positions itself as a premium device in the handheld gaming market. This price is considerably higher than the base model Steam Deck, which starts at a lower price point, making the Ally X a more significant investment. However, buyers get a lot for their money in terms of raw power and advanced features. The high refresh rate display, powerful internal hardware, and customizability make the ROG Ally X a compelling choice for those who want top-tier performance in a portable format.

That said, the steep price might be a barrier for some, especially when considering that the Steam Deck offers a more affordable alternative. While the

Ally X brings more to the table in terms of hardware, not every gamer may feel the need to pay a premium for features like the 120Hz screen or the extra RAM, particularly if they're looking for a more casual handheld gaming experience.

Ultimately, the ROG Ally X justifies its price with its advanced features and performance capabilities, but it's not the most budget-friendly option. Gamers who are willing to invest in a high-performance handheld device will find the Ally X to be a strong contender, but those looking for a more affordable solution might lean toward the Steam Deck or even the Legion Go, depending on their specific needs and priorities.

Chapter 7: Software Experience

Running Windows 11 on a handheld device like the ROG Ally X offers both remarkable flexibility and some notable challenges. On one hand, having a full desktop operating system allows the device to do far more than just play games. It opens up access to a wide range of software, services, and features that you simply wouldn't find on a more closed-off system. This makes the ROG Ally X not just a gaming handheld but also a portable computer capable of handling a variety of tasks, from streaming and browsing to light productivity.

The ability to run multiple storefronts is a big draw for many gamers. Unlike more restrictive systems that lock you into a single platform, Windows 11 lets you access games from Steam, Epic Games, Xbox Game Pass, and more, all in one place. This flexibility is one of the primary advantages of using a desktop OS on a handheld device. For gamers who don't want to be limited by one ecosystem, this kind of freedom is invaluable. It also means you can take advantage of mods and other community-driven enhancements that may not be available on more restrictive platforms.

However, with this power comes complexity. Setting up a Windows 11 device is far from the plug-and-play experience that many gamers are accustomed to with consoles or even other handhelds. The process can feel like setting up a new laptop, complete with account creation, updates, and all the typical overhead that comes with a desktop OS. This complexity is compounded by the presence of bloatware. Like many new Windows devices, the ROG Ally X comes preloaded with apps and features that aren't necessarily relevant to gaming. Things like trial software, news widgets, and various system tools can clutter the interface and detract from the streamlined experience that most handheld gamers expect.

Bloatware isn't just an annoyance; it can also impact performance. While it's possible to remove much of this unnecessary software, it takes time and effort—time that could be spent gaming instead. Additionally, because Windows 11 is designed for desktops and laptops, not handheld devices, it comes with a range of features that simply don't make sense in a gaming context. For example, system notifications, productivity apps, and even the Co-Pilot assistant feel out of place on a device like this, where the focus is supposed to be on gaming.

Another drawback is that Windows 11's interface isn't optimized for smaller screens or touch controls. Navigating menus, adjusting settings, and managing tasks can be cumbersome without the precision of a mouse and keyboard. While the ROG Ally X does have physical controls, interacting with the Windows desktop interface often feels clunky compared to a purpose-built gaming OS. Tasks that would be simple on a larger screen become more challenging in this compact form factor.

Despite these drawbacks, the trade-offs may be worth it for gamers who value versatility over simplicity. The ability to run full-fledged PC games on a handheld device is a huge advantage, and for some, the added complexity of a desktop OS is a small price to pay for that level of freedom. In the end, Windows 11 on the ROG Ally X is a double-edged sword: it provides unmatched flexibility but also brings along the complications of running a desktop OS on a portable gaming device. For those willing to put in the effort, the rewards are significant, but it's not the seamless experience that a dedicated gaming OS might offer.

Armory Crate is the built-in game management software that Asus has developed for the ROG Ally X, and it plays a crucial role in managing the gaming experience on the device. This software serves as the hub where users can access their games, customize performance settings, and monitor system stats. It's a handy tool that tries to bridge the gap between the flexibility of Windows 11 and the user-friendliness of a dedicated gaming OS like SteamOS. However, despite its functionality, it doesn't quite reach the same level of polish or integration that SteamOS provides.

One of the main benefits of Armory Crate is that it consolidates a lot of the device's functionality into one place. Gamers can easily launch their games from various storefronts like Steam, Epic Games, or Xbox Game Pass without having to navigate through Windows 11's traditional desktop environment. The software also provides access to important settings like performance modes, allowing users to tweak the device's power output and fan speeds with just a few clicks. For those who enjoy customizing their gaming experience, this level of control is invaluable, as it allows for real-time adjustments based on the needs of the game or the user's preferences.

However, compared to SteamOS, Armory Crate still feels a bit clunky. SteamOS was designed from the ground up as a gaming-focused operating system, and it shows in its seamless integration with the Steam library and its intuitive interface. Everything about SteamOS is geared toward making gaming the priority, from quick game launches to simple navigation. Armory Crate, on the other hand, is still tethered to the underlying complexity of Windows 11, which can make it feel less streamlined in comparison. There's an extra layer of management involved, and while Armory Crate does a good job of simplifying things, it doesn't quite eliminate the friction that comes with using a full desktop OS.

One area where Armory Crate shines is in its customization options. Users can tweak performance settings, adjust fan speeds, and monitor temperatures directly from the software. This level of control is something that SteamOS doesn't offer to the same extent, making Armory Crate a powerful tool for those who want to optimize their device for different gaming scenarios. However, this depth of customization comes with a trade-off in simplicity. For gamers who just want to pick up and play, the number of options can feel overwhelming, and it's easy to get bogged down in settings instead of focusing on gaming.

Looking to the future, there's certainly room for Asus to improve the software experience by developing a more gaming-focused OS. One of the biggest opportunities for improvement lies in creating a system that prioritizes gaming above all else, similar to what SteamOS has achieved. A dedicated gaming OS could streamline the user interface, reduce the presence of irrelevant features, and eliminate much of the bloat that comes with Windows 11. By focusing solely on the gaming experience, Asus could create a more seamless and intuitive environment that minimizes distractions and maximizes performance.

Such an OS could also integrate Armory Crate's best features, like the performance customization options, into a more cohesive and user-friendly package. Ideally, it would retain the flexibility of Windows 11 for those who want it, but offer a simplified, gaming-first interface that makes the device easier to use out of the box. Asus could also look into better integration with popular gaming storefronts, ensuring that games are easier to access and manage, without the need to switch between multiple platforms.

The potential for a dedicated gaming OS that combines the best of both worlds—a streamlined interface with deep customization options—would make the ROG Ally X an even more compelling choice for gamers. It would reduce the barriers to entry for casual players while still catering to the enthusiasts who want to fine-tune every aspect of their gaming experience. In the end, the ROG Ally X's success in the future may depend on how well Asus can continue to refine and evolve its software to meet the needs of a broad range of gamers.

Chapter 8: The Buyer's Guide

The ROG Ally X is a device that appeals to a specific kind of gamer—someone who values flexibility, power, and portability all wrapped into one sleek package. While it's a powerful gaming handheld, it isn't necessarily for everyone. The ideal audience for the ROG Ally X tends to fall into a few key categories, primarily centered around gamers who want a high-quality experience on the go without sacrificing the performance they've come to expect from their desktop or console setups.

First and foremost, casual gamers who still crave the flexibility of playing AAA titles in a more relaxed, portable format will find the ROG Ally X particularly appealing. These are gamers who might no longer have the time to sit for hours in front of a traditional gaming setup but still want the option to enjoy high-quality gaming experiences in short bursts. Whether they're sneaking in a quick session during a commute, relaxing in bed after a long day, or traveling frequently, the Ally X offers the flexibility to play from virtually anywhere.

Another key audience is those who want power in their handheld experience but also appreciate the versatility of a full Windows operating system. For gamers who are comfortable navigating a desktop OS and want access to multiple gaming platforms—whether it's Steam, Epic Games, Xbox Game Pass, or even older PC games—the Ally X offers something unique. It caters to those who don't want to be locked into a single gaming ecosystem and value the ability to switch between platforms with ease. This audience appreciates the ability to use the device for more than just gaming, whether that's streaming, browsing the web, or even tackling light productivity tasks.

Additionally, the Ally X is a solid choice for tech enthusiasts and performance-driven gamers who enjoy customizing and optimizing their gaming experience. The device's powerful hardware and customization options, like performance mode adjustments through Armory Crate, make it a playground for those who like to tinker with settings to get the most out of their games. For gamers who enjoy tailoring their gaming experience to match specific needs—whether that's balancing battery life for longer sessions or maximizing performance for more graphically intense games—the ROG Ally X offers the tools to do so.

That said, the ROG Ally X may not be the best fit for everyone. Gamers who prioritize simplicity, ease of use, and a plug-and-play experience might find the setup and maintenance required with a Windows-based device a bit overwhelming. Those who are primarily looking for a straightforward handheld gaming experience, without the need for extensive customization or multi-platform access, might lean more towards devices like the Nintendo Switch or Steam Deck, which offer more streamlined, gaming-focused operating systems.

In summary, the ROG Ally X is ideal for casual gamers who want the flexibility to game on their own terms without sacrificing performance. It's perfect for those who value versatility and power in a handheld, and it caters to tech-savvy users who enjoy customizing their gaming experience. While it's not the right device for everyone, for the right audience, it delivers a robust and rewarding gaming experience that stands out in the handheld market.

When considering the ROG Ally X, buyers should be prepared for an experience that blends high performance with the flexibility of a full Windows 11 system, but also comes with the complexity and price tag that accompany such a setup. Managing expectations is key to fully appreciating what the device has to offer and avoiding any potential disappointments.

First, the setup process is more involved than with a typical gaming console. Since the ROG Ally X runs on Windows 11, users should expect a setup similar to a new laptop or desktop PC. This means going through the usual Windows configuration steps, such as signing into a Microsoft account, installing updates, and removing any pre-installed bloatware that might clutter the system. It's not the most streamlined experience for a handheld gaming device, especially when compared to competitors like the Nintendo Switch or Steam Deck, which are designed for a more out-of-the-box, gaming-first setup. Gamers who are comfortable with Windows will find this manageable, but it's worth noting for those who expect a more traditional console experience.

In terms of performance, buyers can expect top-tier capabilities for a handheld device. The AMD Ryzen Z1 Extreme chip and 24GB of RAM provide enough power to run most AAA titles at respectable settings, offering a portable gaming experience that rivals many full-sized gaming laptops. However, this performance comes with some trade-offs. Battery life can vary significantly depending on the power mode and game being played, so it's essential to manage expectations around how long you can game on a single charge. When using Turbo mode for demanding games, expect around two hours of playtime, while lighter games in Silent or Performance mode can stretch the battery life much further.

The price point of $799 places the ROG Ally X in the premium category for handheld gaming devices. Buyers should be aware that they're investing in a powerful piece of hardware with advanced features, but it's also a significant financial commitment. For gamers who prioritize top-notch performance and flexibility, the cost may be justified, but those looking for a more budget-friendly option might consider alternatives like the Steam Deck, which offers a more affordable entry into handheld gaming, albeit with less power.

To enhance the experience with the ROG Ally X, several accessories can be considered. A protective case is a must for gamers who plan to travel with the device frequently. Given the premium nature of the Ally X, protecting it from drops and scratches is a smart investment. Additionally, a dock or stand can be helpful for those who want to use the device for longer gaming sessions while plugged into a monitor or TV. This can turn the handheld into a more versatile gaming station, allowing for a console-like experience when at home.

An extra charger or portable battery pack is also worth considering, especially for gamers who spend a lot of time on the go. Given the variability in battery life depending on the game and performance mode, having a backup charging solution can keep the device running for longer sessions without the worry of running out of power. And for those who want to get the most out of their gaming experience, consider investing in a higher-quality microSD card for expanded storage, as modern games tend to eat up space quickly.

In conclusion, buyers of the ROG Ally X can expect a powerful and flexible gaming device with a few trade-offs in terms of setup complexity and battery life. Accessories like cases, docks, and additional chargers can further enhance the experience, making the device even more versatile for gamers who are frequently on the move. With the right expectations and gear, the ROG Ally X can provide a gaming experience that's hard to match in the handheld market.

Chapter 9: Customer Support and Warranty Issues

In the past, Asus has faced some challenges when it comes to customer service, particularly around warranties and returns. There were numerous reports from buyers who encountered delays in processing returns, difficulties in getting warranty claims approved, and overall frustration with the support process. These issues were concerning, especially for customers investing in high-end products like the ROG Ally X, where reliable support is a key part of the overall experience. For a device at this price point, any shortcomings in customer service can understandably make potential buyers wary.

However, Asus has recognized these concerns and has been actively working to improve its support and warranty processes. In response to the feedback, they have committed to revamping their customer service operations, making it easier for buyers to get the help they need when something goes wrong. This includes clearer communication around warranty policies, faster response times, and more streamlined procedures for returns and repairs. Asus has also taken steps to ensure that their customer service teams are better equipped to handle issues with premium devices like the ROG Ally X, which often require more specialized attention.

Despite these improvements, buyers should still be prepared to take some proactive steps to protect their investment. First and foremost, it's important to thoroughly understand the warranty terms when purchasing the ROG Ally X. Knowing what is and isn't covered can save a lot of frustration if something goes wrong down the line. Registering the product with Asus as soon as you receive it is a good first step, as it ensures that your device is on record should you need to file a claim.

Keeping documentation, including your receipt and any communication with customer service, is also essential. This will help streamline the process if you do need to engage with Asus for a repair or replacement. Additionally, if you encounter any issues with the device, addressing them promptly is important. Waiting too long could result in complications or even a voided warranty, depending on the nature of the problem.

For buyers who want extra peace of mind, considering third-party warranty options or extended coverage plans might be worthwhile. These can offer additional protection beyond the standard manufacturer's warranty, providing more comprehensive coverage for potential issues.

In summary, while Asus has had past concerns with customer service, they have shown a commitment to improving their processes and providing better support for premium products like the ROG Ally X. By being proactive and informed, buyers can better navigate any potential issues and ensure that their investment is well protected.

Conclusion

The ROG Ally X represents a significant step forward in the evolution of handheld gaming. It bridges the gap between powerful, desktop-level gaming and the portability that modern gamers crave. As the gaming industry continues to grow, the demand for devices that allow players to enjoy high-quality experiences on the go will only increase. The Ally X, with its impressive performance capabilities and the flexibility of a full Windows 11 system, is a glimpse into what the future of handheld gaming could look like—where gamers are no longer confined to stationary setups or limited hardware but can carry their entire gaming world with them, wherever they go.

Throughout this book, we've explored the various facets of the ROG Ally X, from its powerful internal hardware to its versatile software features. We've delved into the pros and cons of running Windows 11 on a handheld, the flexibility provided by Armory Crate, and the importance of understanding what this device offers compared to its competitors. While the Ally X is not without its challenges, it is a standout device for those who value performance and customization in a portable format. It's an investment in high-quality gaming on the go, catering to a specific audience that wants the best of both worlds—power and portability.

As you consider whether the ROG Ally X is the right choice for you, it's essential to weigh the factors that matter most to your gaming experience. If flexibility, power, and the ability to customize your gameplay are your priorities, then this device might be the perfect fit. On the other hand, if you value simplicity and a more straightforward gaming experience, alternatives like the Steam Deck might better suit your needs. The key is to make an informed decision based on your own preferences and gaming habits.

We invite you to share your own experiences with the ROG Ally X. How has this device impacted your gaming life? Have you found new ways to enjoy games on the go, or discovered any unique features that stand out to you? Join the conversation, explore related content, and let your voice be part of the ongoing dialogue about the future of handheld gaming.

www.ingramcontent.com/pod-product-compliance
Lightning Source LLC
Chambersburg PA
CBHW061052050326
40690CB00012B/2585